# Contents

## Other Books in the Series

A Natural Beautiful You
Series

# Creating
# Your Own
# Body Butter

MONIQUE JOINER SIEDLAK

Oshun
Publications

**Cover Design by MJS**

**Cover Image by photosforyou@ pixabay.com**

**Published by Oshun Publications**

www.oshunpublications.com

Want to learn about African Magic, Wicca, or even Reiki while cleaning your home, exercising, or driving to work? I know it's tough these days to simply find the time to relax and curl up with a good book. This is why I'm delighted to share that I have books available in audiobook format.

Best of all, you can get the audiobook version of this book or any other book by me for free as part of a 30-day Audible trial.

Members get free audiobooks every month and exclusive discounts. It's an excellent way to explore and determine if audiobook learning works for you.

If you're not satisfied, you can cancel anytime within the

trial period. You won't be charged, and you can still keep your book. To choose your free audiobook, visit:

**www.mojosiedlak.com/free-audiobooks**

# WANT TO BE FIRST TO KNOW?!

# JOIN MY NEWSLETTER!
MOJOSIEDLAK.COM/SELF-HELP-AND-YOGA-NEWSLETTER

# Introduction

Whether you're in the midst of the coldest winter, sizzling under the hot summer sun, or hanging out at home in a controlled environment, the elements can take a severe toll on our skin. This is no small matter! Extreme temperatures and constant climate change—even how we heat and cool our homes dry and distress our skin, causing discomfort or acceleration in the aging process.

Sometimes, despite our best efforts, we just can't seem to recapture that youthful, glowing, plump, or well-hydrated skin. Dry, flaky skin instantly ages a person. If the skin goes unprotected and lacks hydration over time, it'll lose elasticity and be much more prone to fine lines and dull tones. Unfortunately, the products and processes we're treating our skin may actually be part of the problem!

With every drugstore, big-box store, and Instagram "new and improved" product ad, how is a person to know if what they're doing is actually beneficial for their skin in the long run?

I want to suggest that rather than make this more complicated than it needs to be, we go back to simplicity, back to the basics, and yes: back to nature. In this book, I'll give you a foundational understanding of what body butter is, how to use it, and how to make it yourself. You'll find a base recipe for body butter, and learn how to customize it with excellent essential oils.

I know that you're reading this book because you want improved, natural skincare for yourself. once you discover body butter and how to make and customize it, I'm sure you'll be getting requests from friends and family for your "secret recipe!" Whether you tell them or not is up to you, but I think you'll want to share the love.

ONE

# The Importance of Skincare

"EAT AN APPLE AND WASH YOUR FACE": THIS IS SAGE ADVICE for the simple routines and comforts we crave. While proper skin care is probably a little more complicated than this, we won't overcomplicate it here! The more natural and more you enjoy your skincare routine, the easier it will be to sustain it and reap the benefits.

You may have learned that the skin is an entire body system and is considered an organ. Interestingly enough, it's the largest organ in the human body! The average adult has eight pounds of skin, all of it deserving love, attention, and healthy maintenance (Skin and How It Functions, 2017).

Before we get into skincare basics, let's talk about skin and learn what's going on in this incredible human system. Our skin consists of three unique layers: the epidermis, the dermis, and the hypodermis. The epidermis itself comprises up to five layers, depending on where it is on your body. For instance, heels and palms have more layers. This fact is why the skin seems "thicker" here! These epidermal layers are continually moving and regenerating. The innermost layer slowly surfacing as outer layers shed off the skin.

This epidermal layer is the one that we pay most attention to, as it is the one we see, feel, and can treat most readily. While essential oils and some other substances penetrate all three layers of the skin—entering the bloodstream—most of the skincare we'll concern ourselves with here will impact this outer layer, the epidermis.

Basic Care: Cleaning and Hydrating

Essential skincare consists of cleaning and hydrating: that's it. If you've visited your local drugstore, pharmacy, or stepped into a high-end cosmetics boutique, you'd never believe this is true! There must be a million and one ways to tend to these straightforward tasks.

Now, of course, our skin is as unique as we are. Some people naturally tend to have skin that produces more oils, while some tend to have skin that's quite dry. We may have rosacea, acne, or eczema—our skin changes as we age, as well. Most people associate breakouts with the teenage years, but look out: many women discover that first gray hair only to see a pimple pop up the same day. I know, it's not fair!

On top of all this, we may have differing skin tendencies on different parts of our bodies! As we discuss essential skincare, we'll need to take into account our unique skin tendencies.

Cleaning and Hydrating Neutral Skin

You'll notice I didn't say "normal" skin because what is that, anyway? I'll use the word "neutral" to describe skin that isn't over oily or overly dry. To effectively clean neutral skin, use a gentle cleanser. If you love natural everything, try warming a cotton cloth in a bit of water, dropping a bit of sweet almond oil on top, and cleansing with this warm, fragrant indulgence. Press lightly on closed eyes and wipe to the eye's outer edge to remove makeup and refresh delicate skin. The fragrance will become part of your routine: either sending you off to sweet dreams or calming you for the day

ahead. Also, on neutral skin, the oil will serve as a light moisturizer under your SPF barrier.

If you don't love the idea of using an oil to wash, try a
non-soap cleanser like Cetaphil. It is odorless and extremely
easy on the skin, leaving it feeling fresh and plumped.

Follow your cleansing routine with refreshing hydration.
Choose from natural wonders such as coconut oil or avocado
oil, both available in the food section of most supermarkets!

Cleaning and Hydrating Oily Skin

Cleaning skin that tends to produce oil is only a little more
complicated. The most important piece of advice is perhaps
counter-intuitive, and it's simply this: don't overdo it. Scrub-
bing and stripping oily skin only encourages your unique skin
to produce even more oil! So yes, you'll need to be sure to wash
your face in the morning and evening. However, avoid harsh
cleansers and the tendency to scrub. Use an oil-free wash, and
in between, try blotting papers to gently absorb any excess oil.

You may want to try washing with a dilution of apple
cider vinegar several times a week to balance your skin's pH.
Rinse thoroughly when you're finished!

Finish off with an effective moisturizer. Yes, oily skin needs
some type of moisturization, too. As we discussed earlier, we
don't want to strip or irritate this especially sensitive skin type.
Try just a few drops of jojoba oil—warmed in your palm—
and then apply with clean hands in a thin layer across your
skin.

Cleaning and Hydrating Dry Skin

The key to cleaning dry skin is to be gentle, gentle, and
more gentle. This is actually correct for all skin types, but
especially perhaps for dry skin. A mixture of olive oil and
vegetable glycerin makes an excellent, natural cleanser that
will remove dirt and refresh your skin at the same time.

We're keeping it simple, remember? You'll love it when
you hear that you'll follow your cleansing routine with some

of the same ingredients! Moisturize with olive oil when you wake in the morning and coconut oil before bed at night.

The Body

The skin, of course, is much more than just the face. It seems that for such a vital organ, we tend to overlook its care far too often. Body care certainly includes cleaning, but it can consist of so much more!

Consider a routine that includes dry brushing in the morning. Dry brushing uses a soft brush, aiding in exfoliation, and stimulating the lymphatic system. If you want to add a bit of oil to your dry brush—making it, technically, not dry—you'll want to do this before you shower.

While we may not all use—or have even heard of—body brushing, we likely all bathe regularly. Cleansing the body in the bath or the shower is a necessary task, and it should be a delightful one! Choose a water temperature that is slightly cooler than you might like. This temperature change may take some getting used to, but steaming hot water for long periods is extremely drying to the skin as well as the hair. This is especially true if you shower in the morning—a cooler shower is a great way to naturally perk up and welcome your alert mind to the day ahead.

Use cleansers that do the job, but avoid harsh soaps or scrubs. Glycerin-based soaps are naturally hydrating and usually carry simple, natural fragrances. If you crave a little more pick-me-up at the beginning of the day, consider a tea-tree wash: I guarantee you to feel awake and ready when you're done! Washes made with lavender and oatmeal are skin-soothers and are helpful right before bed. Use a clean cotton washcloth as a base for your cleanser on areas that could use a little exfoliation. Also, use a simple squirt of body wash or soap on your hands for everywhere else. Toweling off is another great opportunity to brush away dead skin and reveal the fresh, youthful skin underneath.

Once you're bathed and exfoliated, it's time to add

delectable, protective moisture back into the skin. While there are many ways to moisturize our bodies, I'm going to focus on the carrier I love best and the subject of this book: body butter. In the next chapters, we'll learn what it is and why it's such a unique and powerful moisturizer.

TWO

# What Is Body Butter?

BODY BUTTER IS A VERY THICK, WHIPPED COMBINATION OF occlusives, emollients, and humectants. Body butter often includes several essential oils for both fragrance and specific purposes, such as relaxation-enhancing, energizing, or strengthening.

Emollients are substances that fill in minute crevices and smooth the skin. Humectants attract moisture from the air and draw them into the skin. Occlusives seal all this hydrated goodness and capture it the epidermis.

Some examples of natural emollients include sweet almond oil, olive oil, argan oil, shea butter, or cocoa butter. A couple of natural humectants are more commonly-known ingredients such as glycerin and aloe vera. Simultaneously, beeswax, avocado oil, and cocoa butter are examples of well-known natural occlusives.

Unlike lotion—which is in a liquid form and offers only light skin hydration—body butter is rich, creamy, and ultra-moisturizing. With all those excellent ingredients, each playing their own unique part, body butters are top tier for developing soft, smooth, hydrated, and healthy skin all over your body.

Benefits of Body Butter

Because of it's thick, lush composition, body butter is best suited for just after a shower and just before bed. Think of it as a luxurious treat for world-weary skin—an overnight balm that pays off with a morning glow.

Though body butter has excellent benefits on the skin, I don't recommend using body butter on your face. It's just too rich and has such great staying power that you'd find it impossible to wear makeup over the top: it would likely feel a bit greasy during the day. However, to be sure, use it everywhere else!

Dry off after your warm bath or shower, taking a little extra time to gently exfoliate. Do this by stretching your towel tight between two hands and pulling it back and forth across all of your skin. It's now time to nurture and refresh our skin, having just removed flaky bits of the epidermis and revealing the glowing, new skin underneath!

You'll love to slather body butter on the hardest working parts of your body: knees, elbows, feet, and hands. Work it into the larger areas of the skin as well. These are the thighs, buttocks, belly, arms, and chest. Now, it's pretty tough—downright impossible—to reach your own back with body butter. However, I beg of you. Please find someone to do this for you! Our backs seem to be the most neglected parts of us. when dense, creamy body butter is applied, we can almost hear the skin whisper, "thank you!"

Tucked in bed, you'll only be aware of the lovely sensation of being nurtured, pampered, and healthy. While you sleep, the ingredients of a good body butter go to work repairing and rejuvenating so that when you awake, all of you feels that much more ready to face the day!

THREE

Base Ingredients for Your Body Butter

THE BASE OF ANY SUITABLE BODY BUTTER IS CREAMY, FAT
emollients, humectants, and occlusives. We discussed these a
bit in Chapter 2. We will take a deeper dive here, exploring
my favorite ingredients for healing DIY body butters.

Shea Butter

Shea butter is the shea nut's fat, which grows on shea trees
across Africa's savannah belt. The resulting cream has a
constellation of properties that makes it effective for the skin
and excellent in body butters. Shea fat has no fewer than five
fatty acids, led by a generous 40-60% composition of oleic
acid (Wikipedia Contributors, 2019). Oleic acid, when
combined with linoleic acids, creates a compound that is anti-
inflammatory and naturally healthy for the skin. It's our lucky
day: shea fat comes with a complementary dose of linoleic
acids as well, making it a nourishing and whole product!

Shea stands out as an emollient and humectant because it
melts at "skin temperature," meaning that the epidermis
readily absorbs it (Wikipedia Contributors, 2019). It is chock
full of Vitamin A and is known to reduce skin blemishes, heal
eczema, and reduce wrinkles' appearance. Shea also contains
a fair amount of Vitamin E, which may reduce free-radicals

and aid in micro-circulation (American Shea Butter Institute, 2014).

When purchasing a shea butter, be sure to look for a product that is Grade A and unrefined: this is the purest, most carefully processed state, with the fats extracted by water. Other grades use harsh chemicals to remove the fat, and as such, are not desirable.

Cocoa Butter

Cocoa butter is often interchangeable with shea butter. Still, research points out that shea butter is richer with nutrients and potential benefits for the skin. While the benefits of cocoa butter are less notable, it's worth including in your body butter for two important reasons: it feels incredible, and it smells a little like chocolate (S. Watson, 2017). Cocoa butter comes from the fats in a cocoa bean—yes, the same source of delicious, creamy chocolate. It's very high in fat content, yielding a decadent, skin-loving butter which is even slightly sweet to the taste. Choose raw cocoa butter, which has been minimally processed, for all the fat and flavor benefits.

Coconut Oil

Coconut oil is everywhere, contained in almost everything! Seriously: you can use it to make chocolate candy, bake, sauté, shaving your legs, and even giving your partner a relaxing massage!

Similarly to shea butter, the best quality coconut oils are unrefined and cold-pressed. If you absolutely hate the smell of coconut, choose organic refined coconut oil. You'll have many of the benefits and none of the scent.

Coconut oil is marvelously moisturizing; studies have shown that it's even effective and safe in reducing eczema symptoms (Agero & Verallo-Rowell, 2004, p. 109). It's antimicrobial, amplifies collagen production, and aids in healing the skin (Nevin & Rajamohan, 2010). Keep a tub in the bathroom, use coconut oil on your hands before you go to bed, tame stray hairs, and remove face makeup!

Because it has become so simple to source high-quality coconut oil, this ingredient will be a staple in many of your DIY body butters.

Jojoba Oil

Harvested from the Jojoba tree's seeds, which grows in Southwestern American deserts, jojoba oil is a unique and powerful natural substance. It's a lightweight liquid that is typically known as a "wax ester" rather than an oil. It functions to retain moisture in the skin, and also serves to deliver moisture to the skin! Its composition is very similar to the natural oil—sebum—produced in the human body. Some speculate that using jojoba oil can help keep our bodies' oil production stay in balance (Lepp, 2018).

Grapeseed Oil

Now, here's a fun fact: grapeseed oil is a byproduct of making WINE! Apparently, we can feel even better about our moderate wine consumption because it's all for a good cause: grapeseed oil (Watson, 2018).

Regardless of its origins, grapeseed oil packs a powerful punch. Let's go down the list: antimicrobial, anti-inflammatory, antioxidant, treats acne, softens skin, improves skin elasticity, evens skin tone, and prevents some sun damage (Watson, 2018). Wow! That is truly remarkable: as always, choose a high-quality oil. Just a few drops in your body butter will make a significant impact on your skin.

Sweet Almond Oil

Is it ok if I say that the thing I like best about sweet almond oil is the scent? It's light, nutty, floral, and it just makes me happy. Of course, there's more to the story: I just happen to really like the smell! Sweet almond oil is unique in that it doesn't really penetrate very deeply into the skin. It works as a moisturizer and an emollient right on the epidermis's surface, smoothing, and soothing dry, flaky skin (Daniels, 2020).

Sweet almond oil will be a special ingredient in your body butter recipes. It will add an enjoyable fragrance, several layers of hydration, and smoothing to the other oils and butters you use.

Vegetable Glycerin

This next choice is one of my favorite secret weapons. It's a favorite because it has immediate and long-lasting hydrating effects on the skin. It's also a secret weapon because, well, what in the world is vegetable glycerin? Aside from the fact that it used to be a key ingredient in dynamite, vegetable glycerin is a humectant. It might remind you of a syrup: it's a clear, thick, liquid: slightly sweet to the taste. Natural, or "vegetable" glycerin comes from plant oils, such as coconut oil or soybean oil.

Even a one-time use of vegetable glycerin will "not only smooth the skin but also make it more supple" (Overgaard Olsen & Jemec, 1993, pp. 404 - 406). Because it's a humectant, it attracts moisture—it seems that this process builds over time. Regular use has a tremendous effect on even the roughest skin.

FOUR

About Essential Oils
_____

Wʜɪʟᴇ ᴇssᴇɴᴛɪᴀʟ ᴏɪʟs ᴀʀᴇ ɴᴏᴛ "ᴇssᴇɴᴛɪᴀʟ" ᴛᴏ ᴍᴀᴋᴇ ᴏᴜʀ Body Butter, they offer tremendous benefits. Not only because of their aromatherapeutic qualities but also because of their medicinal properties.

Essential oils come from plants. It may take several pounds of plant material to yield just one bottle of essential oil. Now you see why they can be so very expensive! Essential oils come from petals, leaves, bark, and fruit (John Hopkins Medicine, 2019). What a beautiful gift of nature!

Which Oils Should I Use?

Just as there are more plants, trees, and grasses than we can count, there are many different essential oils. For the purpose of our DIY body butter, I'm going to focus on three categories. However, I do encourage you to explore the full variety of essential oils and find what you like best!

For Relaxation and Stress Relief

•Lavender

○As with all essential oils, be sure to choose high quality, pure lavender oil. doTERRA, Young Living, Vitruvi, Aura Cacia, Plant Therapy, and Rocky Mountain Oils are among the most reputable providers.

○ Pure lavender oil is aromatherapeutic, so the very scent of it in your body butter can soothe migraines and relieve tension.

○ Lavender oil has been shown to motivate skin regeneration and wound healing (Koca Kutlu et al., 2013). Not only will it smell divine, but it will work a bit of magic on your skin.

● Cedarwood

○ Cedarwood has a fresh, earthy scent that is calming and centering. Who wouldn't want to feel transported to a silent grove, ground scattered with pine needles, and the air fresh with pine and sun?

○ Again, the fantastic aroma is only one part of the equation. Cedarwood is antimicrobial and anti-inflammatory, too.

● Frankincense

○ Spicy and earthy, a bit of frankincense can round out the relaxing tones of your body butter. It might actually soothe your aching joints as well—some studies link the use of frankincense to the relief of rheumatoid arthritis symptoms (Etzel, 1996).

For Energy

● Wild Orange

○ Zesty, refreshing, and sweet, this essential oil is favorite among users. It instantly cheers and brightens the day. A body butter made with wild orange and cocoa butter might be too much perfection: you'll have to remind yourself not to lick it off of your hands!

● Lemon

○ Lemon oil is said to be a pick-me-up aromatic—even a little sniff from the bottle can change your perspective on the day. Pair with coconut oil for a sensual, summery body butter.

● Peppermint

○ Peppermint oil is another favorite among aromatherapy aficionados. Along with lavender, it also seems to have indications against migraines. A small whiff can do a little to clear the sinuses but certainly does a lot to boost the mood and increase attentiveness. Peppermint body butter is incredibly fun around the holidays and makes a perfect winter-time gift!

For Youthful Skin

- Tea Tree
  ○ Tea Tree oil is quite potent: never use it directly on skin or around the eyes. With that said, it's a skincare powerhouse. Tea tree oil is highly antibacterial. So much so that it's considered a decent hand sanitizer. It's useful for moisturizing dry skin and reducing inflammation in blemishes. Because it creates a bit of warmth and 'tingle' on the skin, it's best to use just a few drops in any body butter.

- Geranium
  ○ Geranium oil has astringent properties and is fantastic for speeding up the healing of small blemishes. It has a very 'green' plant aroma, which not everyone likes. Others love the fresh-cut, natural scent.

- Ylang Ylang
  ○ Ylang-ylang may be most well known for its supposed aphrodisiac properties; unfortunately, those are not well documented. Nevertheless, it really is a wonderful essential oil. It's a highly floral fragrance and found in many top-shelf perfumes. I love it because of its linalool. A compound found in ylang-ylang that makes it antifungal, antibacterial, and anti-inflammatory.

Cautions

Oils are potent: this is why they can make a meaningful and positive impact on our skin's health. Below are some tips and cautions that go along with using them.

- Always use a carrier oil when you apply essential oils to your skin. Carrier oils are light oils that dilute the essential oil and make it possible to use just a drop or two to spread across your skin. Suggested carrier oils are: fractionated coconut oil, jojoba oil, sweet almond oil, and grapeseed oil.
  ○ Consider doing a test patch on your skin, blending a

carrier oil, and the essential oil you want to use in your body butter.

- A recommended dilution ratio is 15 drops of essential oil to 1 ounce of carrier oil (National Association for Holistic Aromatherapy, n.d.).

- Some oils are not recommended for pregnant women because they can cross the placental barrier. If you are pregnant or want to give body butter to someone who is, avoid these oils:

  o Aniseed, basil, birch, camphor, clary sage, hyssop, mog wort, oakmoss, parsley seed or leaf, pennyroyal, peppermint, rosemary, rue, sage, tansy, tarragon, thuja, thyme, winter-green, and wormwood (Mashack, n.d.).

- While essential oils do not get moldy or musty, they change over time due to oxidation. The introduction of oxygen happens when you open your bottle! As such, oils do have expiration dates. The good news is that they range from a two-year shelf life to an eight-year shelf life (Hagen, 2019). Since you'll be using your oils in wonderful body butters, you shouldn't have to worry too much! When in doubt, however, check a shelf life chart, usually provided by essential oil distributors.

FIVE

## Basic Whipped Body Butter Recipe

AND NOW—THE MOMENT WE'VE ALL BEEN WAITING FOR! YOU understand quality ingredients, how they function, and what kinds of unique variations you can integrate into your DIY body butter. All you need is a base recipe, and I'm about to share just that!

Remember that body butters are infinitely customizable, but I want to start with something straightforward that you can use as a template for your own experimentation! The formula is essentially three parts solid oil or 'butter' and one part light oil for each of these recipes. Of course, we'll be adding fun variations along the way, but this is all you really need to have for pure, nourishing body butter!

Base Recipe

Ingredients:

• 1 1/2 cups of any solid oil or butter (coconut oil, shea butter, or cocoa butter)

• ½ cup of any light oil (jojoba, grapeseed, or sweet almond)

Instructions:

•Carefully melt solid oils (fats) until they just reach a liquid state.

○ Do this in a large microwave-safe dish in the microwave, melting 12 seconds at a time, and stirring in between.

○ This can also be done in a "bain-marie," meaning that you place the solid oil into a small pot. Then placing that pot over another pot filled with water and simmering on the stove.

▪ The purpose of melting the oil is to create a consistent texture in your final product.

● Pour all of the melted oil into a mixing bowl, and let cool on the counter for 10 minutes.

● Place the bowl in the refrigerator for a minimum of one hour.

○ The goal here is to return the melted oil to a semi-solid state so that you can whip it into a butter!

● Once the oil is solid but soft—you should be able to easily press a finger into it—grab a hand mixer or scrape into the bowl of your stand mixer. You know what to do: whip it!

● When the butter is whipped into a delightful, creamy froth, place the bowl back in the fridge to set the whip a bit— 15 minutes should be enough.

● Use a spatula to scrape it out and into one or two lidded glass jars.

○ You can upcycle and reuse jelly jars, or pick up a box of small mason jars at the store.

● Keep the butter in a cool, dark place. If you live in a very warm climate, you will need to store it in the fridge and bring it out to soften a bit before use.

Customization Example

Ingredients:

● 1/2 cup cold-pressed, unrefined coconut oil (use refined if you don't like the smell of coconut)

● ½ cup Grade A shea butter

● ½ cup raw cocoa butter

● ½ cup sweet almond oil

● 1 Tbsp vegetable glycerin

- 2 tsp arrowroot powder: this will give the body butter a smoother, less greasy feel
- 15 drops of your favorite essential oil

Instructions:

*These instructions are similar, but not the same as those for the base recipe. I'll put an asterisk next to the new information

- Carefully melt solid oils until they just reach a liquid state.
  - Do the melting in a large microwave-safe dish in the microwave, melting 12 seconds at a time, and stirring in between.
  - This can also be done in a bain-marie.
    - The purpose of melting the oil is to create a consistent texture in your final product.
- Pour all of the melted oil into a mixing bowl, and let cool on the counter for 10 minutes.
- *Add sweet almond oil
- *Add vegetable glycerin
- *Add essential oils
- Place the bowl in the refrigerator for a minimum of one hour.
  - The goal here is to return the melted oil to a semi-solid state so that you can whip it into a butter!
- Once the oil is solid but soft—you should be able to easily press a finger into it—grab a hand mixer or scrape into the bowl of your stand mixer. You know what to do: whip it!
- *Add arrowroot powder
- When the butter is whipped into a delightful, creamy froth, place the bowl back in the fridge to set the whip a bit— 15 minutes should be enough.
- Use a spatula to scrape it out and into one or two lidded glass jars.
  - You can upcycle and reuse jelly jars, or pick up a box of small mason jars at the store.

●Keep the butter in a cool, dark place. If you live in a very warm climate, you will need to store it in the fridge and bring it out to soften a bit before use.

SIX

## Recipes

IN THIS SECTION I HAVE INCLUDED SOME OF THE RECIPES I'VE
worked on. I like scents that a bit strong so I would suggest a
bit of trial and error to get the strength you prefer.

### Cooling Night Face Cream

- 10 drops Frankincense Essential Oil
- 10 drops Lavender Essential Oil
- 5 drops Lemon Essential Oil
- 5 drops Cedar Wood Essential Oil
- 5 drops Tea Tree Essential Oil

**Perfect for the face.**

### Lemon Drop Body Butter

- 35 drops Lemon Essential Oil

**Note: Lemon essential oil can cause skin sensitivity. Be careful using this one if you're going outside in the sun!**

## Lavender Body Butter

- 35 drops Lavender Essential Oil

## Peppermint Body Butter

- 30 drops Peppermint Essential Oil

**Excellent for foot and leg care.**

## Tranquility Body Butter

- 20 drops Lavender Essential Oil
- 10 drops Vetiver Essential Oil
- 5 drops Sandalwood Essential Oil

## Upbeat and Positive Body Butter

- 20 drops Wild Orange Essential Oil
- 10 drops Grapefruit Essential Oil
- 5 drops Spearmint Essential Oil

## Mystical Rejuvenation Body Butter

- 15 drops Frankincense Essential Oil
- 10 drops Cedar Wood Essential Oil

- 10 drops White Fir Essential Oil

## Pumpkin Pie Body Butter

- 15 drops Cinnamon Essential Oil
- 10 drops Ginger Essential Oil
- 10 drops Clove Essential Oil

## Spring Breeze Body Butter

- 15 drops Rosemary Essential Oil
- 15 drops Lemon Essential Oil
- 10 drops Grapefruit Essential Oil

## Fresh Flowers Body Butter

- 15 drops Ylang Ylang Essential Oil
- 15 drops Jasmine Essential Oil
- 10 drops Lavender Essential Oil

## Romance Body Butter

- 15 drops Jasmine Essential Oil
- 15 drops Neroli Essential Oil
- 10 drops Rose Essential Oil

## Energizing Body Butter

- 15 drops Grapefruit Essential Oil
- 15 drops Peppermint Essential Oil

- 10 drops Bergamot Essential Oil

## Smooth and Silky Body Butter

- 20 drops Frankincense Essential Oil
- 20 drops Lavender Essential Oil

## De-Stress Me Body Butter

- 20 drops Lavender Essential Oil
- 10 drops Lime Essential Oil
- 10 drops Mandarin Essential Oil

## Oriental Bloom Body Butter

- 20 drops Grapefruit Essential Oil
- 10 drops Vetiver Essential Oil
- 5 drops Ginger Essential Oil

## Heavenly Scent Body Butter

- 20 drops Patchouli Essential Oil
- 10 drops Grapefruit Essential Oil
- 5 drops Ylang Ylang Essential Oil

## Romance Body Butter

- 15 drops Sandalwood Essential Oil
- 5 drops Clary Sage Essential Oil
- 5 drops Ylang Ylang Essential Oil

- 5 drops Coriander Essential Oil
- 4 drops Patchouli Essential Oil
- 4 drops Frankincense Essential Oil
- 2 drops Vetiver Essential Oil

## Orange Creamsicle Body Butter

- 30 drops Mandarin Orange Essential Oil
- 10 drops Vanilla Essential Oil

## Strawberry Fields Body Butter

- 30 drops Strawberry
- 10 drops Vanilla Essential Oil
- 5 drops Musk Essential Oil

## Moon Goddess Body Butter

- 20 drops Sandalwood Essential Oil
- 10 drops Lemon Essential Oil
- 5 drops Rose Essential Oil

## Citrus Flower Body Butter

- 20 drops Frankincense Essential Oil
- 10 drops Lemongrass Essential Oil
- 10 drops Ylang Ylang Essential Oil

## Garden Musk Body Butter

- 20 drops Lime Essential Oil
- 10 drops Fennel Essential Oil
- 10 drops Patchouli Essential Oil

## Simple Waters Body Butter

- 20 drops Patchouli Essential Oil
- 15 drops Frankincense Essential Oil
- 10 drops Grapefruit Essential Oil

## Conclusion

Body butters done right are part of healthy skin care. Providing moisture, humectants, emollients, and therapeutic oils to our skin. Making your own body butter at home gives you full control over the ingredients, sourcing, the quality, and the amounts. This allows you to experiment and tweak your recipe until it's just what you like.

Once you have a small stockpile of the base ingredients, I encourage you to slowly add some of the "extras" to your inventory. Such as a variety of light oils, a sampling of essential oils, vegetable glycerin, etc. Try making several variations at a time so that you can compare and contrast for the next time.

Small four-ounce mason jars make a perfect size for generous samples and gifts for birthdays, anniversaries, and more! I'm confident that once you start creating and using your own body butter that you'll start talking them up to your friends, and they'll want some, too! You might want to name your creations: they are, after all, your unique contributions. Naming them gives you a chance to describe what you really feel with the body butters: "Plumping Peppermint Polish" or "Lush Lemon Luxury" anyone?

With all the endless variety of big-box skincare options from who knows where, made of who knows what, I think you'll really love the connection you have to nature and to your body when you create and use your very own body butters. Mix them up, slather them on, soak them in, and your skin and spirit will thank you. Enjoy!

# References

Agero, A. L. C., & Verallo-Rowell, V. M. (2004). A Randomized Double-Blind Controlled Trial Comparing Extra Virgin Coconut Oil with Mineral Oil as a Moisturizer for Mild to Moderate Xerosis. Dermatitis (Formerly American Journal of Contact Dermatitis), 15(03), 109. https://doi.org/10.2310/6620.2004.04006

American Shea Butter Institute. (2014). 21 Reasons to Use Shea Butter | American Shea Butter Institute. Sheainstitute.Com; American Shea Butter Institute. https://www.sheainstitute.com/asbi-library/21reasons/

Amplitude Magazin. (2019). Woman Applying Lotion. In Unsplash. https://unsplash.com/photos/B9xBxClDgBQ/info

Daniels, L. (2020, April 29). Almond oil for skin: How to use it and benefits. Www.Medicalnewstoday.Com; Healthline Media. https://www.medicalnewstoday.com/articles/almond-oil-for-skin#benefits

Etzel, R. (1996). Special extract of BOSWELLIA serrata (H 15) in the treatment of rheumatoid arthritis. Phytomedicine, 3(1), 91–94. PubMed. https://doi.org/10.1016/s0944-7113(96)80019-5

Hagen, T. (2019, January 7). Do Essential Oils Expire? Shelf Life, Expiration Dates & Tips. Blog.Planttherapy.Com; Plant Therapy Essential Oils. https://blog.planttherapy.com/blog/2019/01/17/do-essential-oils-really-expire/

Hume, C. (2018). Essential Oils. In Unsplash. https://unsplash.com/photos/0MoF-Fe0w0A/info

John Hopkins Medicine. (2019). Aromatherapy: Do Essential Oils Really Work? John Hopkins Medicine; The John Hopkins University. https://www.hopkinsmedicine.org/health/wellness-and-prevention/aromatherapy-do-essential-oils-really-work

Koca Kutlu, A., Çeçen, D., Gürgen, S. G., Sayın, O., & Çetin, F. (2013). A Comparison Study of Growth Factor Expression following Treatment with Transcutaneous Electrical Nerve Stimulation, Saline Solution, Povidone-Iodine, and Lavender Oil in Wounds Healing. Evidence-Based Complementary and Alternative Medicine, 2013, 1–9. Hindawi. https://doi.org/10.1155/2013/361832

Lepp, D. (2018, May 22). 5 Easy Ways to Use Jojoba Oil. Botaneri; Botaneri, LLC. https://botaneri.com/easy-ways-to-use-jojoba/

Mashack, C. (n.d.). Essential Oils and Pregnancy Safety. Www.Morelandobgyn.Com; Moreland OB-GYN Associates, S.C. Retrieved October 1, 2020, from https://www.morelandobgyn.com/blog/essential-oils-and-pregnancy-safety

National Association for Holistic Aromatherapy. (n.d.). NAHA | Exploring Aromatherapy. Naha.Org; National Association for Holistic Aromatherapy. Retrieved October 1, 2020, from https://naha.org/explore-aromatherapy/about-aromatherapy/methods-of-application/

Nevin, K. G., & Rajamohan, T. (2010). Effect of topical application of virgin coconut oil on skin components and antioxidant status during dermal wound healing in young rats. Skin Pharmacology and Physiology, 23(6), 290–297. https://doi.org/10.1159/000313516

Overgaard Olsen, L., & Jemec, G. B. (1993). The influence of water, glycerin, paraffin oil and ethanol on skin mechanics. Acta Dermato-Venereologica, 73(6), 404–406. https://doi.org/10.2340/0001555573404406

Skin and How It Functions. (2017, January 18). National Geographic; National Geographic Society. https://www.nationalgeographic.com/science/health-and-human-body/human-body/skin/#close

Watson, K. (2018, February 7). Grapeseed Oil for Skin. Healthline; Healthline Media. https://www.healthline.com/health/grapeseed-oil-for-skin

Watson, S. (2017, March 30). Cocoa Butter: Benefits, Uses, and More. Healthline; Healthline Media. https://www.healthline.com/health/beauty-skin-care/cocoa-butter-benefits

Whelan, C. (2020, February 10). Ylang Ylang Essential Oil Uses & Benefits. Healthline; Healthline Media. https://www.healthline.com/health/ylang-ylang#benefits

Wikipedia Contributors. (2019, July 23). Shea butter. Wikipedia; Wikimedia Foundation. https://en.wikipedia.org/wiki/Shea_butter

# About the Author

Monique Joiner Siedlak is a writer, witch, and warrior on a mission to awaken people to their greatest potential through the power of storytelling infused with mysticism, modern paganism, and new age spirituality. At the young age of 12, she began rigorously studying the fascinating philosophy of Wicca. By the time she was 20, she was self-initiated into the craft, and hasn't looked back ever since. To this day, she has authored over 40 books pertaining to the magick and mysteries of life.

To find out more about Monique Joiner Siedlak artistically, spiritually, and personally, feel free to visit her **official website**.

www.mojosiedlak.com

facebook.com/mojosiedlak

twitter.com/mojosiedlak

instagram.com/mojosiedlak

pinterest.com/mojosiedlak

bookbub.com/authors/monique-joiner-siedlak

## More Books by Author

**Practical Magick**
Wiccan Basics
Candle Magick
Wiccan Spells
Love Spells
Abundance Spells
Herb Magick
Moon Magick
Creating Your Own Spells
Gypsy Magic
Protection Magick
Celtic Magick
Shamanic Magick

**African Magic**
Hoodoo
Seven African Powers: The Orishas
Cooking for the Orishas
Lucumi: The Ways of Santeria
Voodoo of Louisiana
Haitian Vodou

Orishas of Trinidad
Connecting with your Ancestors

**Personal and Self Development**
Creative Visualization
Astral Projection for Beginners
Meditation for Beginners
Reiki for Beginners
Manifesting With the Law of Attraction
Stress Management
Time Bound
Healing Animals with Reiki
Being an Empath Today
Get a Handle on Anxiety

**The Yoga Collective**
Yoga for Beginners
Yoga for Stress
Yoga for Back Pain
Yoga for Weight Loss
Yoga for Flexibility
Yoga for Advanced Beginners
Yoga for Fitness
Yoga for Runners
Yoga for Energy
Yoga for Your Sex Life
Yoga: To Beat Depression and Anxiety
Yoga for Menstruation
Yoga to Detox Your Body
Yoga to Tone Your Body

## Last Chance
## Join My Newsletter!

If you missed it, I have a free gift available for you and wanted to remind you it's still available.

mojosiedlak.com/self-help-and-yoga-newsletter

Thank you for reading my book.
I really appreciate all your feedback and would love to hear what you have to say! Please leave your review at your favorite retailer!